LE CORBUSIER

© 2004 Assouline Publishing for the present edition
601 West 26ᵗʰ Street, 18ᵗʰ floor
New York, NY 10001, USA
Tel.: 212 989-6810   Fax: 212 647-0005
www.assouline.com

First published by Assouline, Paris, France
All works by Le Corbusier © Adagp, Paris 1998

Color separation: Gravor (Switzerland)
Printed by Grafiche Milani (Italy)

ISBN: 2 84323 419 0

LE CORBUSIER

ÉLISABETH VÉDRENNE

ASSOULINE

1e Corbusier: no architect in the world is more famous. He is considered the architect of the century. He represents modernity. A man of the future, forever changing, a visionary. Above all, Le Corbusier was a creator. His work as painter, sculptor, architect, city planner, writer and theoretician was both exaggeratedly praised and unfairly mocked. Every contemporary architect is indebted to him, for better and for worse. During his lifetime, they flocked from every corner of the earth to work with him, sometimes without pay, in his agency, the Atelier 35 S, on Rue de Sèvres. The man was intimidating. The smooth face of a Buddhist priest, thick round glasses, the eternal bowtie, he looked like a dandy, reserved yet simple in his ways. Called the "fada" ("nut") in Marseilles, his aristocratic, direct manner fascinated people. His remote gaze, uncommunicative ways, fits of anger and abrupt tone did nothing to attenuate his disciples' devotion. He was admired despite his crazy demands, his absences, his moralizing tone, and his cutting statements that annoyed people but hit the nail on the head. He was venerated for his nonconformist ideas, wild utopias, flashes of genius, his way of constantly projecting himself forward – in short, for his freedom. Inventing was his master word: never copy, always innovate. "Dare and want to create," he would say. A dreamer, he would sometimes get lost in the clouds, be unrealistic, exaggerate, and sometimes go too far, as with his absurd Plan Voisin, in which no less than the Marais, one of the most beautiful neighborhoods in Paris, was to be leveled! His projects perpetually disturbed every academism, and in France especially, they faced fierce opposition. Le Corbusier long terrorized the right-minded bourgeoisie with his wonderful tremors.

Many simply see him as the inventor of the very worst in architecture! He is accused of have sired horrible high-rises, strip buildings, decrepit housing projects in nightmarish urban neighborhoods, in short, of all the mistakes and blunders of post-war reconstruction and the aberrations of the 70's-80's. Wrong: everything that is good about contemporary architecture, we owe to him. He invented a style that has transformed our lives, a style that is now so much a part of our lives that we cannot imagine it could ever have been revolutionary: bright duplex apartments, airy and bathed in light, fluid movement and acoustic comfort, large volumes emphasized with little furniture, sober and elegant, tricks to enlarge space, incorporate elements, decks, rooftop gardens, etc. Today, none of this sounds special. Before Le Corbusier, there was no such thing!

A self-taught man

Le Corbusier was a mountain man. Charles-Edouard Jeanneret – his real name – was born on October 6th, 1887 in La Chaux-de-Fonds, in Swiss Jura. He developed a deep love of nature and forged an independent mind. After an apprenticeship as an engraver/chaser in the watch-making business, he excelled in drawing at the fine arts school of his home town, read Ruskin, and became familiar with the

Arts and Crafts ideology of the time. He followed a work-study program at Frères Perret in Paris, where he discovered the charms and advantages of reinforced concrete. The compulsory trip to Italy, where he visited the Ema monastery in Tuscany, taught him to appreciate an architectural style suited to the needs of monks; it was to be a lifestyle model for him throughout his career. He traveled throughout Germany in 1910 and even worked six months in the workshop of Peter Behrens, where he met both Gropius and Mies van der Rohe, the two future directors of the Bauhaus. They did not leave a lasting impression on him, but it was there that he understood the need for a partnership between industry and architecture.

His true initiatory voyage was his trip east, a long poetic ramble around the Mediterranean Sea. He drew like mad, did watercolors, fell in love with the cupolas of Venice and Istanbul, jotted down notes, and took an interest in the rural architectural styles of the Balkans. Lastly, in Greece, he was stunned by the monastic life on Mount Athos, and by the Parthenon. This shock provided the seeds for all his future ideas. On one side, the Spartan life of the monks, reduced to the strict minimum, on the other the whiteness of the Acropolis, its geometric precision – square-cube-sphere. These two discoveries were to become the symbol of his idea of harmony. Back in Switzerland, he went to work, building individual houses, and already thinking about low-cost housing projects. His training was brief and unsystematic, but this culture of the self-taught man, heterogeneous and rich, based on his personal experience of seeing, and the way he used his drawings as his memory, turned him into an incredibly free architect! Those "things seen" were to remain essential. Le Corbusier was never to be an office man. He was a highly physical architect, and an artist. The Chapelle de Ronchamp, for example, a mature work, is a mosaic of echoes, poetic fragments, and remnants of his wanderings through the Mediterranean countryside.

From among those marvels buried in his subconscious, we find his periscopes, wells for letting in the light which light up the chapel from above, directly inspired by the Serapeum of the Adriana villa in Tivoli. These correspondences and resonances nourished him to the end. So how can anyone claim that Le Corbusier despised the past and wanted to set off on a clean slate? The only thing he rejected was conservatism.

Purism and Esprit Nouveau

At the age of thirty, he took his destiny into his own hands and decided to move to Paris. Who was Charles-Edouard Jeanneret (he did not become Le Corbusier until he began so sign the articles he wrote with that name for his publication *L'Esprit Nouveau*, created in 1920) when he met the painter Amédée Ozenfant? A man heading into the future. A humanist combined with a "machinist" who believed in industry and the future of the machine: "We have to learn to see not a bird or a dragonfly in an airplane, but a flying machine." For this architect, machines have only qualities. They symbolize perfection, precision, purity, economy, and efficiency. When he invented his expression "living machine," he disturbed a lot of people. Few understood that he simply meant a house that is as convenient, efficient and attractive as an airplane or a car. At that time, Le Corbusier was seeking to assert himself. A forerunner here too, he understood that one must "communicate," as we say today. He used his love of writing to serve the adventure of purism, presenting it in his magazine *L'Esprit Nouveau*. Ozenfant and Le Corbusier opposed "purism" to "cubism" and the various "futurisms:" a purer painting, in both the moral and figurative sense, simpler, underlined by a more precise

8

structure. A rational, ordered art, often representing still lives of everyday, anonymous objects: a subtle balance of bottles, piles of plates, siphons, etc., juxtaposed in a composition of light colors. It was Ozenfant who taught Le Corbusier about oil painting. But they broke up in 1925, the student, as usual, surpassing the master. Le Corbusier continued to paint, adding volume, in a more voluptuous style, combining "poetical reaction objects" with organic forms – seashells, bones, fossils, pebbles, pine cones, etc. – until gradually a woman's body emerged. At this time, he was close to Léger and Picasso. He was to paint his entire life, in the morning, in his studio, specially designed in 1934 in his apartment at 24 rue Nungesser-et-Coli. It was his secret laboratory and he even claimed: "It is through the channel of painting that I came to architecture."

Man's happiness

Purism promoted a new attitude. It heralded a new civilization for a new man with a new spirit. Le Corbusier sought to "provoke an intellectual emotion." Hence, emotion and mind are put on the same level. This duality, this mixture of intellect and senses is a typical facet of the Le Corbusier approach. He was interested in life, in its complexity and totality. From beginning to end, his credo was: build, but to make people happy. What may seem demagogical today was in fact very sincere. "The important thing is to reestablish or establish harmony between Man and his environment." The detail is inseparable from the whole, just as the outside is inherent in the inside. According to Charlotte Perriand, he wanted to "create Man's nest and the tree to bear it." These injunctions to "live better" may sound paternalistic and authoritarian. But without this engine, would he have succeeded in moving the mountains he had to move to impose this lifestyle (both individual and collective), which is the foundation of our current way of life? History was to weaken his belief in a wonderful tomorrow and in the machine. A more spiritual, perhaps mystical vision of architecture was to follow.

Against decorative art

At the Exposition des Arts Décoratifs in 1925, Le Corbusier presented his L'Esprit Nouveau pavilion, a true revolutionary manifesto (as his Temps Nouveau pavilion was to be in 1937 at the Exposition Internationale in Paris). Le Corbusier's proposals hit like a bombshell. His pavilion was divided into two parts. The first part was devoted to housing and made of standard elements. The second part was educational, presenting urban planning projects that made more than one visitor's hair stand on end. In general, he was criticized for what was considered excessive bareness. André Levinson, in *Demeures Françaises*, compared his pavilion to the antechamber before the Père Lachaise cemetery! Le Corbusier was already applying his future furnishing program to the letter in his "housing cell:" "compartments, chairs, tables." In short, the bare minimum. The walls, livened up with paintings by Léger, Ozenfant and himself, were sparkling white: "Each citizen is requested to replace his wall upholstery, damask, wallpaper and stencils with a coat of Ripolin paint. You cleanse your home... Then you cleanse yourself." A startling approach, and not very popular among Art Deco lovers, who would have sold their soul for rosewood, ebony and macassar, for knobby growths and thorns, and for stylized rose bouquets. Naturally, Le Corbusier was alluding to Emile-Jacques Ruhlmann, Süe and

Mare, and their followers. For him, beauty did not come from something being rare or precious, and certainly not from ornamentation, since "decorating camouflages." Luxury is elsewhere. "Cheap things are always abundantly decorated; a thing of luxury is well made, unadorned and clean, pure and sound, and its bareness reveals its qualities." A contemporary, the Bauhaus in Weimar, professed the same ideas. As for the architect, he let loose in his book *L'Art Décoratif d'Aujourd'hui*, where he predicted: "The virtually hysterical rush these past ten years toward orgiastic decoration is simply the last spasm of a foreseeable death." His critics compared his "bare" style to that found in hospitals and military barracks. In his pavilion, Le Corbusier, who had not yet developed the famous furniture he was to create soon after with Pierre Jeanneret and Charlotte Perriand, used existing furniture, already practically mass-produced, everyday items, archetypes that had proven their worth. He furnished it with the famous turned wood armchair, the *B9* model, by Thonet, that was to be found everywhere, even in his home, and with standard painted wood compartments, which he combined to form either storage shelves or walls to separate interior spaces.

1930's furniture

In 1927, Le Corbusier began to take an interest in variable-position furniture such as tilting dentist chairs and colonial rocking chairs. He became enthused with metal, an interest shared with many other members of the avant-garde of that time. Marcel Breuer had just designed his first steel tube chair. Le Corbusier made sketches of lounge chairs, blueprints of what was to become the most famous lounge chair of the XXth century, the *B306*. At first made by Thonet, it was remade by Cassina starting in 1965, as were the other furniture items in this series. Thus began ten fruitful years for the Le Corbusier-Pierre Jeanneret-Charlotte Perriand team.

The collaboration with Charlotte Perriand was decisive. She handled the drawing of the furniture and the organization of the interior design. Energetic and sensitive, she was good at finding practical solutions: "Le Corbusier was waiting – impatiently – for me to breathe life into the furniture." She selected the materials and the craftsmen, developed the prototypes and always succeeded in implementing the master's wishes. In this way, the now mythical metal and tubular furniture was born, presented for the first time at the 1929 Salon d'Automne. Items included the swivel chair, the bathroom stool, the extendable table, and the "sling chair," as well as the fauteuil grand confort, a large cube of metal and leather that has come to symbolize the modern armchair! In charge of furnishing all the lodgings, Perriand "equipped" all the "purist" villas of the 1930's, and later in the 1950's, the famous Unités d'Habitation (housing units) in Marseilles, Rezé-les-Nantes and elsewhere, in addition to the houses at the Cité Universitaire de Paris. She was behind the development of the prototype – highly innovative at the time – for the "bar-kitchen" or "living room-kitchen," with the service hatches and automatic garbage chutes, and the sanitary facilities. Again, it was Perriand who sought to make the furniture more popular and more affordable: she covered their frames with cloth or elastic fabric, and began to use straw wood and raffia. She perfected metal "compartments" with their infinite number of combinations, and fine-tuned the concept of multifunctionality. During that time, Corbusier was becoming increasingly fascinated with textures: the "skin" of concrete, and the pony skin of his armchairs. He liked the way fur gave warmth to linoleum, the slabs of Saint-Gobain opaque white glass that filtered light, and the tabletops made of black slate. All this

1930's furniture, with its interchangeable and stowable forms, evoked nomadic life, while the materials, aside from steel, were reminiscent of nature. Le Corbusier the visionary foresaw what our lifestyle would be: "We have become "nomads" living in apartments and houses that will be equipped with common services: we will change apartments as our families evolve... We will sometimes change our circumstances, our neighborhood too, etc."

Five Points toward a new architecture

The "Five Points toward a new architecture" appear in a text published in 1926, in which Le Corbusier explains the five key concepts underpinning his entire work: free design of the ground plan, free design of the façade, the horizontal window, the supports, and the roof-garden. A new way of conceiving architecture, made possible through the use of reinforced concrete and the freedom of plasticity offered by this magic material that allowed both *"less is more"* – according to the phrase coined by Mies van der Rohe – and the lyrical and exuberant forms of Oscar Niemeyer in Brasilia.

Free design of the ground plan: concrete allows heavy metal slabs to be set on concrete poles forming an independent frame. You can arrange partitions as you like to obtain various architectural "effects," and each floor can be arranged differently. Before that, in stone buildings, everything was dictated by the bearing walls.

Free design of the façade: the skin of the frame, itself derived from the free ground plan. The design of this façade and its openings is free.

Horizontal window: the horizontal openings resemble a strip running from one end of the building to the other, letting in light and providing sweeping vistas.

Supports: an elevating system that raises the building off the ground and purposely avoids the feeling that it is rooted in the earth. These supports – or posts – are like visible roots, exposed to the air. They support the entire structure. They also free the architect from floor surface constraints.

The roof-garden: sloping roofs are a thing of the past! Concrete allows flat roofs. This creates a surface equal to the floor surface, on which you can create a hanging garden or a large terrace. You can even create an "apartment in the air," as the architect designed for Charles de Bestégui.

In 1924, Le Corbusier began to build the Petite Maison for his parents on Lake Leman. He chose a "box laid on the ground" measuring 60 square meters, inexpensive, easy to live in, and poetic. Set facing the sun at the water's level, it was closed in with walls because, he said, if "the landscape is omnipresent... it becomes tiresome." The idea that you have to use things sparingly is a very lecorbuséenne concept: "For a landscape to count, it must be delineated and sized through a radical decision [revealing it] only at strategic points." Like a stage director, he created an opening in the wall surrounding the garden, resulting in a "painting-window" providing a view of the most beautiful spot.

This appeal for "cut-out windows" can be seen in the roof-garden of the Savoye villa. An access ramp is even provided to lead you straight to the hole in the wall, offering a tightly framed view of a piece of the landscape, like the windows painted in portraits from the Italian renaissance. Le Corbusier had a deep love of nature. He constantly strove to highlight it or bring it indoors through his strip windows. Le Corbusier adored the sun – on his skin, as a nudist, true to his mountain puritan background and nonconformist attitude – and on the skin of others, both indoors and outdoors, because to him the sun, like light, meant life. He even invented the brise-soleil

14

("sun-breaker") to enjoy the sun while attenuating it. He often designed solariums in his roof-gardens, closed off with high walls that also act as wind-breakers. His obsession with the sun is obvious in the vast roof-deck of the radiant Cité de Marseille, a child's kingdom hanging in midair, where he planned a nursery school, gymnasium, swimming pool, solarium, running track and man-made hills to play on. A joyful life under the Mediterranean sun, with a view of the sea and mountains. A Virgilian dream. When he designed a hanging garden, he was in fact an ecologist before his time. He tasted the heady feeling of "walking on his roof," strolling through the wild grass which, with its roots, provides a thick moist padding offering insulation from the heat and cold: "The roof-garden lives off itself through sun, rain, wind and the seed-carrying birds."

The Purist villas

In the 1920's, as always assisted by his cousin Pierre Jeanneret, Le Corbusier built four little jewels called the Purist villas: the La Roche villa in Paris, the Stein villa in Garches, the Baizeau villa in Carthage, and the most famous one, to which architects flock from around the world, the Savoye villa in Poissy. These four houses offer a detailed illustration of the "Five Points toward a New Architecture." A subtle game is played between inside and outside in these sculptures-houses. Moving around inside is like traveling through a work of art. You shift from cold to warm, from bright to dark, letting your gaze wander along the long, narrow strip of landscape that unfurls as you advance. You rest your elbow against a wall as if you were leaning on an ocean liner's railing, and admire the ingenious diagonal and curved structures. Everything is fluid and puts one in a meditative state. Everything tends toward movement. *Déambulation*, meaning to stroll, is a key word in Le Corbusier's vocabulary. In all these villas, he includes a ramp system that leads to the upper floors (so do beautiful winding stairs), while their sloping planes actually carve up the space. The ramp is the centerpiece for getting around. He was strongly attached to this "architectural stroll" which constructs the space it generates as you advance. The ramp floor is coated with black slip-proof linoleum. A shelf generally runs along sliding windows, emphasizing the continuous line. It can be used to place a book or vase, or to sit or lean on. These villas, at once abstract and surreal, seem to be out of a dream. They are also called the villas blanches, or white villas.

Color

We saw how important the "Ripolin law" was to Le Corbusier. However, "the interior of a house must be white, but to appreciate this white, a finely tuned polychrome scheme is required." We are less aware of his love of color. In the Purist villas, charron blue, chocolate brown (a heat conductor, he often painted his exposed radiators in this color) and various pastel tones – pearl gray, poussin yellow, buvard pink – are arranged in a pictorial composition. He dared to paint walls red and shelves bright yellow. In his Unités d'habitation, strong colors appear gaily side by side. Outside, colored cubes, as if set into the loggias, make up gigantic palettes. While on the walls the colors are flat, once transposed into glass, they shine. Iridescent fragments like nuggets are set into the walls at the Chapelle de Ronchamp, the Nantes nursery school, and the villas built in India, at Ahmedabad. In 1926, in the Cité Frugès de Pessac, near Bordeaux, he explored a polychrome coating for the outer walls of blocks, arranged head-to-foot. A series of sienna, light ultramarine blue, and pale anglais green facets are strung together as in a prism. Soon afterward, in 1931, for the Salubra company, he created his famous claviers (keyboards) with such pretty names as *Ciel, Espace, Sable, Paysage, Velours and Mur*. Unfortunately, it was not a great success. Unconsciously, the architect gave priority to white, and the infinite tones of gray found in concrete.

The lyricism of concrete

The white architecture of the 20's and 30's had seen its day. After 1950, Le Corbusier took a liking to rough finishes as opposed to smooth ones, and vibrant textures. He was increasingly drawn toward primitive forms. Sensuality reigned, tinged with a subtle mix of surrealism and the Picasso style, on the beautiful floating vessel called the Chapelle de Ronchamp, erected in 1954. This fantastic composition is an entanglement of convex and concave shapes that are virtually expressionist – almost neo-baroque. Le Corbusier "king of the straight line" seems a distant memory. The whiteness of the rough plaster coating, designed to catch and absorb the light, creates a contrast, highlighting the tender gray of the unsurfaced, exposed concrete, which on the contrary reflects the light. The gray roof, a sort of boat or slanted saddle, it too made of concrete, is shaped like a crab shell. The concrete is alive: cast in wood molds, it still bears their traces. With its protuberances reminiscent of a cave and its inlaid glass colored or decorated with cosmological symbols, Ronchamp is an ode to nature and prayer. On the other hand, the concrete of the Couvent des Tourettes tends to evoke stone, that "tough skin."

Le Corbusier began to give free reign to that controlled madness of an artist, making his architecture impossible to categorize. It was later to interest a wide range of architects, such as the Mexican Luis Barragan, the American Louis Kahn, and the Japanese architect Kenzo Tange. In the 1960's, he was far removed from the international style of steel and glass towers. Called to India by the pandit Nehru, in 1951 he began the Shodhan and Sarabhaï villas in Ahmedabad, and built the entire city of Chandigarh, a splendid symphony dedicated to unsurfaced concrete. It allowed him to play with transparency, with reflections using the many expanses of water, with breaks and dissymmetries. Everything seems "off-beat." Ramps and corridors crisscross in monumental style. A strange, extreme world...

The cabanon: the ideal minimum

Along with the Savoye villa, the cabanon at Cap Martin is the most visited Le Corbusier site. Yet it is just a small wood hut of 15 square meters set above the waves. The architect came here to write facing the sea, where he would swim several times a day. In this place, he realized his dream of living like a monk. Everything fits into a square cell with 3.66 m sides that is 2.26 m high – the proportions found in Le Modulor. This cube is the quintessence of his way of life. The few furniture items he designed – two beds at right angles, stool-chests, tables and cabinets in prefabricated wood – delineate the living quarters. The volume is designed to fit each act and each need. The outer walls are covered with "pine slab", and the interior wood panels are left rough, except for the floor, painted yellow, and one panel, painted green. A mural painting warms up the entrance. The ventilation and location of the windows is carefully studied.

Forever controversial and mischievous, he wrote: "My visitors are always scandalized by the toilet bowl that sits in the middle of the room. Yet it is one of the most beautiful objects that industry has ever manufactured." Le Corbusier vanished in the deep blue, facing the sun, on August 27, 1965, in this simple, perfect place.

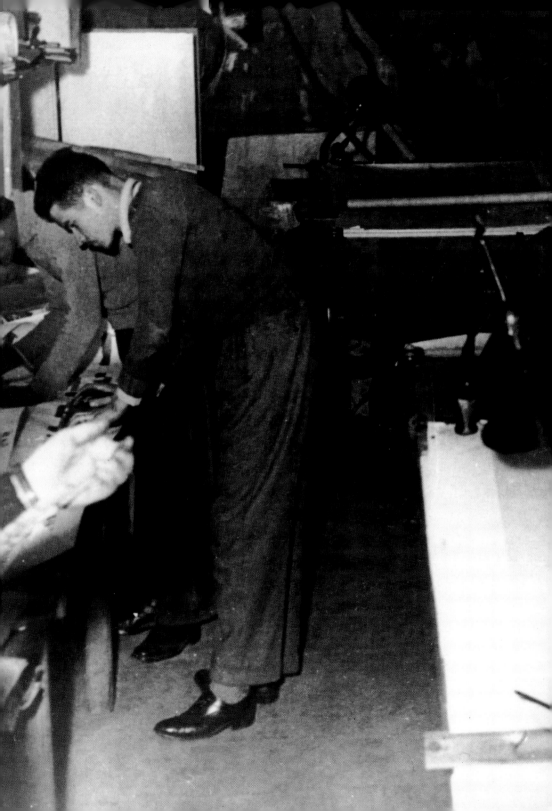

323

L-C
57C 45
F
LC

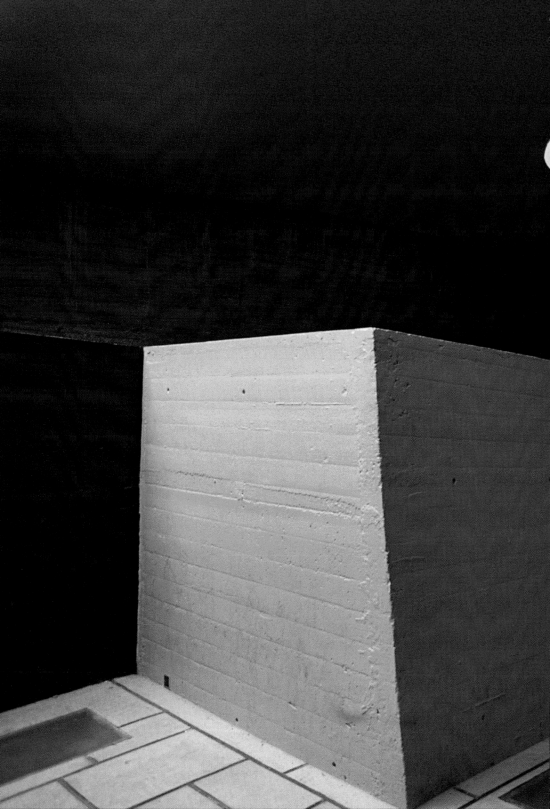

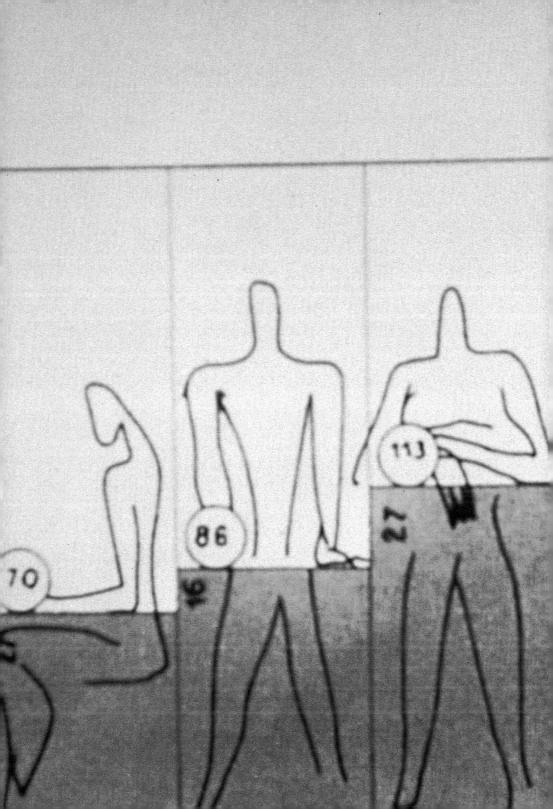

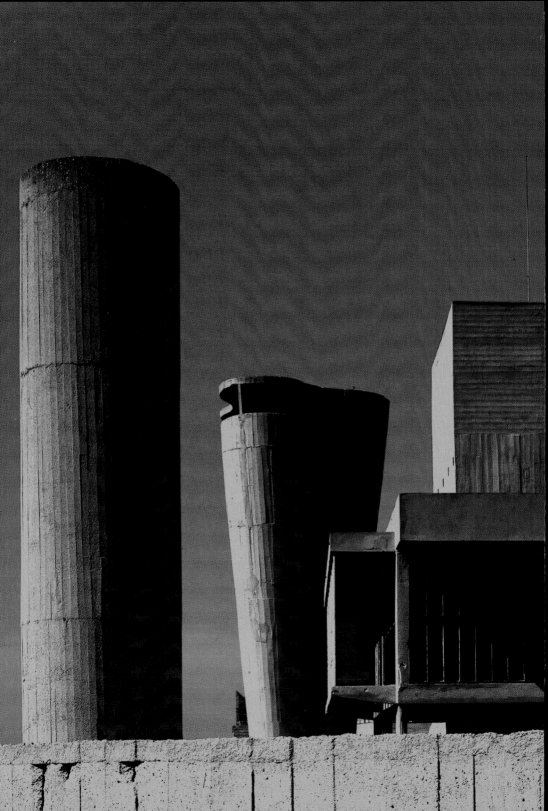

Chronology

1887: On October 6th, Charles-Edouard Jeanneret (later called Le Corbusier) was born in La Chaux-de-Fonds (Switzerland). His father was a watch case enamellist and his mother was a piano teacher. His older brother Albert, for whom he built the Jeanneret-Raaf villa in Paris in 1925, was to become a musician

1901: Takes engraving and chasing classes at the La Chaux-de-Fonds art school.

1807: Begins his travels through Europe.

1808: During his stays in Paris, he meets Henri Sauvage and Eugène Grasset. The latter sends him to work with the Perret brothers, pioneers in reinforced concrete. In Lyons, he meets Tony Garnier.

1910-11: Works five months in Berlin at Peter Berhens with Mies van der Rohe and Walter Gropius. Travels in Central Europe, Greece and the Middle East.

1913: Returns to La Chaux-de-Fonds, where he opens an interior design firm and gets orders for several houses. He leaves definitively end 1916.

1917: In Paris, Auguste Perret introduces him to the painter Amédée Ozenfant. Sharing the same ideas, they will create the Purist movement.

1920: Charles-Edouard Jeanneret takes on the pseudonym Le Corbusier. With Ozenfant, he publishes the magazine *L'Esprit Nouveau*, to which a wide range of writers including Adolf Loos, Elie Faure and Jean Cocteau contribute. This magazine, which combines text and photos in an original manner, gives Le Corbusier international recognition. He paints a lot.

1924: Opens the *Atelier 35 S* at 35 Rue de Sèvres with his cousin Pierre Jeanneret. Several generations of young painters flock to this studio and disseminate his ideas throughout the world.

1925: Builds the *Esprit Nouveau* pavilion at the *Exposition Internationale des Arts Décoratifs* in Paris, and creates a scandal. The pavilion is a true manifesto, marking a break with *Art Nouveau* and *Art Deco*. He draws up the highly controversial Plan Voisin, which will nevertheless influence modern urban planners and prefigure his designs for the *Cité Radieuse*. He publishes *L'Art Décoratif d'Aujourd'hui*, a sort of pamphlet against "decoration" as it is understood at the time.

1927: Charlotte Perriand joins the Atelier 35 S and Le Corbusier entrusts her with interior design. With her (and with Pierre Jeanneret, who too often tends to be overlooked), he creates a series of furniture items that have become classics of modernity. He also publishes "Five Points toward a New Architecture," which, with some variations, he will continue to apply throughout his life.

1928-30: Frequent trips to the USSR and Latin America, where he builds a following.

1930: Obtains French nationality, marries Yvonne Galis, finishes building his Purist villas and discovers North Africa.

Le Corbusier's apartment, 24 rue Nungesser-et-Coli, Paris, 1931-1935.
© *Photo: Robert Doisneau/Rapho, Paris.*

1935: First trip to the United States, with which he is to entertain an ambiguous relationship.

1937: Works in Brazil with Lucio Costa and Oscar Niemeyer.

1938: Exhibits his paintings at the *Galerie Louis Carré* in Paris.

1940: Closes his agency because of the war.

1945: Lays the plans for the *Unité d'Habitation* in Marseilles (called *"la maison du fada"*), an experiment for his *Cité Radieuse*, which is not completed until 1952, thanks to the support of Eugène Claudius-Petit, Minister of Reconstruction and Urban Planning. To the traditional suburban garden cities, he opposes and builds the "vertical garden city." Between 1950 and 1960, he builds several *Unités d'Habitation* in France and even one in Berlin, all as controversial as the one in Marseilles.

1951: Nehru commissions him to build the new capital of Punjab, Chandigarh, on which he again works with his cousin Pierre Jeanneret, but which is not finished at his death. Constructs two villas in Ahmedabad.

1952: Builds his famous *cabanon* on Cap Martin.

1955: Inauguration of the *Chapelle de Ronchamp*, an organic glorification of concrete and one of the most important religious edifices of the XXth century.

1957: His wife dies.

1962: Retrospective exhibition of his paintings and sculptures and at *Musée d'Art Moderne* in Paris.

1965: On August 27th, dies while swimming at Cap Martin.

Bibliography

BENTON, Tim, *Les Villas de Le Corbusier, 1920-1930*. Paris, Philippe Sers, 1984.

FRAMPTON, Kenneth, *Le Corbusier*. Paris, Hazan, 1997.

HERVÉ, Lucien, (photos of), *Le Corbusier, l'artiste, l'écrivain*. Neuchâtel, Griffon, 1970.

JENGER, Jean, *Le Corbusier, l'architecture pour émouvoir*. Paris, Gallimard, "Découvertes," 1993.

Le Corbusier et la Méditerranée. Exhibition catalog of the Musée de la Vieille Charité. Marseille, Parenthèses, 1987.

LUCAN, Jacques (directed by), *Le Corbusier, Une encyclopédie*. Paris, Centre Georges-Pompidou, 1987.

LE CORBUSIER, *Œuvre complète*. Reprint. Zurich, Artémis, 1991. 8 volumes. Consultable at the Fondation Le Corbusier library.

RAGOT, Gilles and DION, Mathilde, *Le Corbusier en France, projets et réalisations*. Paris, Le Moniteur, 1997.

Shodhan villa, Ahmedabad, 1952-1954 – Façade, terrace side
© Photo: O. Wogenski, Paris

Le Corbusier

Le Corbusier at his drafting table. © Photo: Walter Limot/AKG, Paris.
The "Modulor." Lithograph, 1956. New measurement system based on the human scale (man standing and man with arm raised) and its harmonious proportions. The combinations are unlimited. © Fondation Le Corbusier, Paris.

Le Corbusier in his agency, designed lengthwise, located 35 rue de Sèvres, in Paris, in a former Jesuit home. © Keystone, Paris.

LC2 armchair, also called **Fauteuil grand confort**. Le Corbusier, Pierre Jeanneret and Charlotte Perriand, 1928. Black leather and chrome-plated tubes. © Photo: Mario Carrieri, Cassina Spa, Meda.
Le Corbusier and Charlotte Perriand. Rare photograph showing them together at the **Bar sur le toit**, 1928. © Photo: Pierre Jeanneret/documentation Charlotte Perriand.

Table LC6. Le Corbusier, Pierre Jeanneret, Charlotte Perriand, 1928. Glass top and legs in painted airplane tube with egg-shaped sections. Table presented at the Salon d'Automne in Paris in 1929, now recreated by Cassina (Italy). © Photo: Alda Bolo/Cassina Spa, Meda.

La Roche villa, Paris, 1923-1925. Set behind the windowpane of the villa built for the Swiss banker and modern art collector Raoul La Roche, the famous lounge chair **LC4**. The villa is now open to visitors. © Fondation Le Corbusier, Paris.

Unique version of LC4 lounge chair. Le Corbusier, Pierre Jeanneret, Charlotte Perriand, 1928. Original cloth version without its headrest. Chrome-plated steel frame, opaque black lacquered steel base. The chair also exists in colt hide or leather with headrest. Now recreated by Cassina (Italy). Private collection © Galerie Doria, Paris.

Savoye villa, Poissy, 1929. Detailed view of exterior. One of the Villas blanches, called purist villas, characterized by its thin pillars and strip windows. The villa is now open to visitors. © Photo: Frank Eustache/Archipress, Paris.

Savoye villa, Poissy, 1929. Detailed view of terrace. We can clearly distinguish the walkway leading to the window that cuts up the landscape. © Photo: J.C. Ballot/CNMHS, Paris.

Savoye villa, Poissy, 1929. Detailed view of living room. Period furniture, including a very interesting Le Corbusier ceiling light designed entirely lengthwise. © Viollet Collection, Paris.

Savoye villa, Poissy, 1929. Detailed view of bathroom adjoining master bedroom. Recessed bathtub covered with turquoise mosaics, with built-in day bed. The light is zenithal. © J.C. Ballot/CNMHS, Paris.

Church villa, Ville d'Avray, 1928. This other purist villa, furnished by Charlotte Perriand, was destroyed in 1965. Period photo of library. © Fondation Le Corbusier, Paris.

Le Lac villa, Vevey, 1923. Drawing by Le Corbusier in 1945 of the villa built for his parents. Interior view, plan FLC 32305. The 11-meter long window overlooks Lake Leman. © Fondation Le Corbusier, Paris.

Le Corbusier observing the model of the Palais des Soviets (1930). The building was never constructed. © Photo: Walter Limat/AKG, Paris.
Jeanneret villa, Paris, 1923-1925. Detailed view of villa that is now the headquarters of the Fondation Le Corbusier. © Fondation Le Corbusier, Paris.

Modern neighborhood, Frugès, Pessac, 1924-1927. Detailed view of two houses with polychrome exterior facades. Le Corbusier used sienna, light ultramarine blue, pale anglais green and white. © Photos: Bruno Boyer, Talence.

Modern neighborhood, Frugès, Pessac, 1924-1927. Two more of the fifty houses of the garden city designed for the Bordeaux industrialist Henry Frugès. They are gradually being restored according to the strict instructions of the architect. © Photos: Bruno Boyer, Talence.

Assembly house, Chandigarh, (Punjab, India), 1951-1957. Two views of the interior. Le Corbusier played on the contrast between the tender and rough grays of the reinforced concrete and the colored, brilliant enamel of the main door he painted himself. © Photo: O. Wogenski, Paris (left). © Photo: F.X Bouchard/Archipress, Paris (right).

High Court building, Chandigarh, 1952. Bird's-eye view of polychrome interior. The Court of Justice and the secretariat (ministry building) are also part of this neighborhood, called Capitale. © Photo: O. Wogenski, Paris.

Sainte-Marie-de-la-Tourette convent, Evreux-sur-Arbresle, 1953-1960. View of lateral chapel, painted in the bright colors of the convent that Le Corbusier built with his collaborator Iannis Xénakis, the mathematician and musician. You can see a red light gun diffusing light through the roof, and a mitraillette, a source of finer light. © Photo: J. Salmon/Archipress, Paris.

Notre-Dame-du-Haut Chapel, Ronchamp, 1950-1955. A unique work of art, both organic and expressionist, the chapel is the fruit of both Le Corbusier's architectural and sculptural talent. © Photos: O. Wogenski, Paris.

Notre-Dame-du-Haut Chapel, Ronchamp, 1950-1955. Interior. The colored lighting is diffused through multiple openings of various sizes. The stained glass was painted by Le Corbusier. © Photo: Frank Eustache/Archipress, Paris.

The cabanon, Cap Martin, 1951-1952. Detailed view. This hut, whose exterior is coated with pine slabs, overlooks the Mediterranean Sea. It is now open to visitors. © Photo: Hugues Bigo, Paris.

The cabanon, Cap Martin, 1951-1952. Interior. The ideal minimum living cell, whose measurements are based on the Modulor. Plywood panels on the walls and built-in prefabricated furniture. © Photo: Hugues Bigo, Paris.
The Modulor, 1945. Study of Man's most common positions (sitting, standing, leaning) and the resulting measurement system. © Fondation Le Corbusier, Paris.

Salvation Army shelter, Paris, 1933. Its current colors are not those initially wanted by the architect. The shelter is still used. © Photos: Frank Eustache/Archipress, Paris.

Pavillon du Brésil, Cité Universitaire, Paris, 1957-1959. Student bedroom with minimum furnishings chosen by Charlotte Perriand. The curved private shower behind the white wall was a luxury at the time! © Photo: Pignata Monti, Paris.

Unité d'habitation, Marseilles, also called Cité radieuse, 1945-1952. View from vent pipes and elevator tower of the extraordinary roof-garden (left) and view of one of the many "interior streets," behind the glass wall designed to soften the light (right). Experimental city that was revolutionary for France in the 1950's. © Photos: Peter Cook/Archipress, Paris.

Le Corbusier's and his wife's grave, Cap Martin cemetery, 1957. Le Corbusier vanished in the sea in 1965, at the foot of his cabanon. He rests with his wife, facing that same sea, with the symbols of the architectural geometry and art he designed himself. © Photo: O.W., Paris.

The publisher would like to thank for their collaboration Charlotte and Pernette Perriand, as well as Évelyne Tréhin (fondation Le Corbusier).
Thanks are also due to Archipress, Marie-Christine Biebuyck (Magnum), Hugues Bigo, Bruno Boyer, la Caisse nationale des monuments historiques et des sites, Nicole Chamson (Adagp), Isabella Colombo (Cassina), Denis Doria (galerie Doria), Bernard Garrett et Hervé Mouriacoux (AKG, Paris), Lucien Hervé, la galerie François Laffanour-Downtown, Mario Pignata Monti, Rapho, Albert Raymond (Keystone), Roger-Viollet et Olivier Wogensky.
For more information on Le Corbusier and his work, please contact la fondation Le Corbusier, villa La Roche-Jeanneret, 8-10, square du Docteur-Blanche, 75016, Paris (tél. : 01 42 88 41 53).